SPOTLIGHT
ON CHILDREN'S
AUTHORS

RICK RIORDAN

SUE CORBETT

Cavendish
Square

New York

Published in 2014 by Cavendish Square Publishing, LLC
303 Park Avenue South, Suite 1247, New York, NY 10010

Copyright © 2014 by Cavendish Square Publishing, LLC

First Edition

Library of Congress Cataloging-in-Publication Data

Corbett, Sue.
Rick Riordan / Sue Corbett.
p. cm. —(Spotlight on children's authors)
Includes bibliographical references and index.
Summary: "Presents the biography of children's book author Rick Riordan while exploring his creative process as a writer and the cultural impact of his work"—Provided by publisher.
ISBN 978-1-60870-935-9 (hardcover)—ISBN 978-1-62712-143-9 (paperback)—ISBN 978-1-60870-942-7 (ebook)
1. Riordan, Rick—Juvenile literature. 2. Authors, American—21st century—Biography—Juvenile literature.
3. Children's stories—Authorship—Juvenile literature. I. Title.
PS3568.I5866Z57 2013
813'.54—dc23
2012000516

Senior Editor: Deborah Grahame-Smith
Art Director: Anahid Hamparian
Series Designer: Kay Petronio

Photo research by Lindsay Aveilhe
Cover photo courtesy of Sophie Laslett/eyevine/Redux

The photographs in this book with permission and through courtesy of: Amy Sussman/Getty Images: p. 4; Joe Vogan/Alamy: p. 8; HO/RTR/Newscom: p. 10; © 1997 by Rick Riordan. Bantam Books, a division of Dell Publishing.: p. 14; Sophie Laslett/eyevine/Redux: p. 17; Katie Orlinsky/The New York Times: p. 19; Images.com/Corbis: p. 20; Photos 12/Alamy: p. 22; © 2006 by Rick Riordan. Hyperion Books, a division of The Walt Disney Company: p. 24; Bloomberg via Getty Images: p. 25; © 2008 - 2012 Scholastic Inc.: p. 28; Getty Images: p. 30; Photos 12/Alamy: p. 32; Agencia el Universal/El Universal de Mexico/Newscom: p. 34; © Fox 2000 Pictures. All rights reserved./Courtesy Everett Collection: p. 35; Charles Sykes/AP Photo: p. 36; Wirelmage/Getty Images: p. 38

Printed in the United States of America

CONTENTS

INTRODUCTION: Who in the World Is Ransom Reese?............ 4

CHAPTER 1 A Lone Star Childhood..... 8

CHAPTER 2 A Hero Is Born......... 16

CHAPTER 3 Best-sellerdom......... 22

CHAPTER 4 One Door Closes and Another Opens............. 28

CHAPTER 5 Hollywood!.......... 32

CHAPTER 6 What's Next for Rick? 36

Rick Likes to Read:............. 40

Books by Rick Riordan 41

Glossary............. 42

Chronology............. 43

Further Information............44

Bibliography 45

Index............. .46

INTRODUCTION:
Who in the World Is Ransom Reese?

Nancy Gallt is a successful literary agent who receives thousands of letters and manuscripts each year from writers who hope she'll help them get their books published. She gets letters from people she's never heard of on a daily basis.

But one such letter, which she received in 2004, left her scratching her head. It was from a writer named Ransom Reese.

"He said he'd gotten my name from reading Jeanne DuPrau's *City of Ember*—Jeanne had thanked me in the acknowledgments," Gallt remembered. "He said he had written mysteries for adults that had twice won the Edgar Award, but he didn't want to use his real name for this new book because he had written it for kids, not adults." (The Edgar Award, named for Edgar Allan Poe, is a very prestigious award given annually to the best mystery novel of the year.)

In his letter, Reese had included an excerpt from the book that he was hoping Gallt would help him get published. The excerpt, which itself was a letter, began this way:

Dear Mortal Reader:
I have sworn upon the River Styx that the events in this book are purely fictional.
    There is no such twelve-year-old boy as Perseus "Percy" Jackson. The Greek gods are nothing more than old myths. . . .

The letter was signed,

Yours sincerely,

Chiron Kentavros
Immortal Trainer of Heroes
Activities Director, Camp Half-blood

Reese finished his own letter with the phrase "Beware of Greeks bearing gifts," written in Latin.

"I only knew what it meant because I had taken Latin in high school," Gallt said. She was impressed by Reese's query letter, so she asked him to send her his manuscript. "My overwhelming feeling was, 'This guy knows his stuff.'"

By the time she finished reading his manuscript and decided to represent him, Gallt was *really* curious: who in the world was Ransom Reese? She shared the manuscript with her husband, Craig Virden, who at the time was publisher of Random House Children's Books. He, too, was convinced that Ransom Reese had to be a pseudonym for someone who was already famous.

"Craig said, 'This guy's a pro. This is just too well done,'" Gallt remembered. Still, when Gallt called Ransom to say that she would take him on as a client, he insisted that he did not want to give his real name. "He was also extremely calm when I called, which was another indication to me that it was no surprise to him that somebody was interested in his manuscript," said Gallt.

It wasn't until Gallt shopped the manuscript around to publishers that someone insisted on knowing the real identity of Ransom Reese. "There was interest from [many publishers], but during the course of the auction, somebody said, 'If this is a pseudonym, we need to know who the underlying writer is, and we don't think a pen name is a good idea,'" Gallt said. At the time, a writer named Lemony Snicket was already creating a huge stir among young readers by sending his "representative," Daniel Handler, to appearances in his place.

Ransom Reese had to be unmasked. His book *was* going to be published, but he wasn't going to be able to slip into bookstores in his toga for a reading while keeping his true identity—a beloved teacher of middle school English—top secret.

Ransom Reese was, of course, Rick Riordan.

Rick was born in Austin at an auspicious time for Texans—former governor Lyndon B. Johnson was serving as president of the United States.

Chapter 1
A LONE STAR CHILDHOOD

Richard Russell Riordan Jr. was born in San Antonio, Texas, in 1964. He was the only child of two fine artists, both of whom made their living as teachers. Rick's dad, Richard Sr., made ceramics. His mom, Lyn Belisle, taught art in San Antonio's public schools for more than three decades before switching to Trinity University in San Antonio, where she now teaches in the computer science department.

As a kid growing up in South Texas, Rick was known as Ricky. He remembers he "was constantly called Ricky Ricardo," the name of Lucy's husband on the popular 1950s TV comedy show *I Love Lucy*. Rick once posted his second-grade report card on his blog, *Myth & Mystery*. It shows he was a very good student, earning mostly As.

Regarding his report card, Rick wrote, "Lowest marks? PE—no surprise. I never could climb that stupid rope. Conduct—no comment. And writing? B student. Nothing remarkable. My handwriting was lousy. My motivation was nonexistent. My work ethic? I'd rather be outside playing Godzilla and the Smog Monster with my buddies." Nobody, he thought, would have predicted a future for him as a best-selling novelist. "I imagine my teachers would've chuckled at the idea. 'Not likely,' they'd say. 'His penmanship is atrocious and he can't spell.'"

Rick had another high hurdle to clear on his path to becoming a professional writer: he did not like to read. Although his teachers read aloud *Charlotte's Web* and the Boxcar Children books, which Rick enjoyed hearing, picking up a book on his own was perhaps the last thing he chose to do in his free time.

"I remember other kids being excited about reading incentive programs in elementary school, like 'read twenty books and get a gold sticker!' That just left me cold," Rick said in a 2007 interview with children's book blogger Jen Robinson. "I liked comic books and looking at photos in nonfiction books, but the idea of reading a novel was just too daunting. I would get bored easily. Nothing grabbed me."

Rick credits his eighth-grade English teacher, Patricia Pabst, with turning him into a reader. Mrs. Pabst had written her master's thesis on J. R. R. Tolkien's Lord of the Rings trilogy. She introduced these books to Rick.

The book that turned Rick into a reader, J.R.R. Tolkien's fantasy classic, *The Hobbit*

"Tolkien's trilogy opened up the world of fantasy for me," Rick recalled. "Mrs. Pabst showed me how the trilogy was patterned after Norse mythology."

Rick reread the Lord of the Rings books about ten times, kick-starting what would become a lifelong interest in fantasy and mythology, especially Greek and Norse legends. It was after reading Tolkien's masterpieces that Rick, encouraged by Mrs. Pabst, decided to try writing his own stories. Mrs. Pabst was also the first person to suggest he submit a story to a magazine. He got a rejection letter.

"My very first rejection note was from (Isaac) *Asimov's Science Fiction* magazine in 1978," Rick said. "My mother saved this letter for years and brought it out after I got published."

At Alamo Heights High School, Rick was on the newspaper staff, and he won a state award for feature writing. He also showed a mischievous streak: he published an underground newspaper that made fun of the school, especially its losing football team.

"The football team later egged my car," he admitted.

But even in high school, Rick was reluctant to do the required reading. "I basically faked my way through every English class by listening to discussions. I was a good writer, so I could give the teacher a decent essay without ever having read the book," Riordan said in his interview with Robinson. "Of course, my karmic punishment was that I became an English major. I had to go back in college and read all that stuff they tell you to read in high school."

When Rick first set off for college, he had no intention of becoming a writer. His plan was to study music and become a guitar player. Rick's mom, Lyn, was a musician, and he wanted to follow in her footsteps. "I focused most of my creative energy on music, and was lead singer in a folk rock band," he said. The college he chose to attend, North Texas State University, had the best music program in his area. He soon changed his mind, however, and decided to transfer to the University of Texas at San Antonio to pursue a double major in English and history. He kept his musical career alive by playing in bands on the weekends and by working as the music director at a summer camp, Camp Capers, in the Texas Hill Country. (Later, what Rick had learned about cabin life would come in very handy in his writing career, when he created the [fictional] Camp Half-Blood on Long Island.)

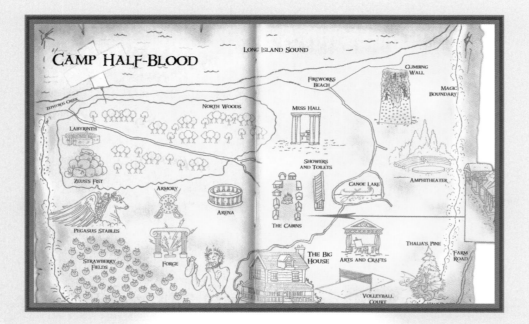

Rick's experience as a music instructor at a summer camp in Texas helped him create Camp Half-Blood, a base for Percy Jackson and the other demigods.

While at the University of Texas, Rick also became a published author. Two of his short stories appeared in the college literary magazine. Despite this success, Rick still did not make writing a career goal. After graduating from college, he followed in his parents' footsteps and became certified to teach English and history in Texas public schools. He also settled down by marrying his high school sweetheart, Becky, whom he had dated since they were fifteen years old.

"After college, I became a teacher, and was quite happy with the idea of doing that the rest of my life," Rick wrote on his website.

Rick might still be a teacher if he had never left Texas. But after a brief stint teaching middle school in South Texas, Rick and Becky left for Northern California, where Rick planned to pursue a graduate degree in medieval studies at San Francisco State University. It was in California that Rick got his first itch to write a novel, in large part because he was homesick.

"I was really missing Texas," Rick said. Though he had read mostly fantasy and science fiction as a teen, he had developed a love of mysteries as a college student. Since graduating, he had written short mystery stories and had even published a few, including one in *Ellery Queen's Mystery Magazine*. As a result, he said, "I decided, on a lark, that I would try writing a hard-boiled private eye novel set in my hometown of San Antonio." His main character was Jackson "Tres" (pronounced "trace") Navarre, a detective skilled in both martial arts and medieval literature. Rick wrote in his spare time and finished the story in ten months. ("It almost wrote itself," he has said.)

"Once I had a completed manuscript, I queried agents. Many said no. One said yes," Rick recalled. "Once I had an agent, she began shopping the manuscript around. Many publishers said no, all for different reasons. Some loved the story and disliked the characters. Some loved the characters and disliked the story. There didn't seem to be any consensus."

Finally, however, the manuscript arrived in the office of Kate Miciak, editorial director of Bantam Dell, a part of the Random House publishing group. Miciak reads a lot of manuscripts very early in the morning, on the bus she takes to commute to Manhattan from her home in western New Jersey.

"This bus is always full of carpenters and electricians who are going into the city to work for the day, and they have this magical ability to fall sound asleep. Waking them up is really a bad thing," Kate said. "So I remember very distinctly reading Rick's manuscript on the bus and trying as hard as I could not to laugh out loud because everybody around me was asleep. I was in love by the end of the first page. I read the whole thing that day and made an offer [to buy it] the next."

Rick was thrilled but, curiously, not surprised. "The strange thing is I had a feeling

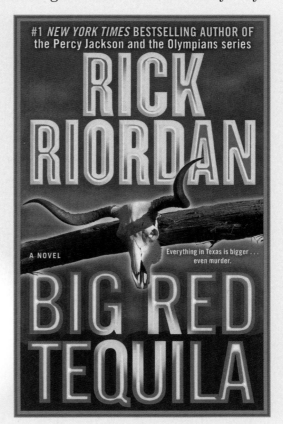

Being homesick for Texas led to Rick's first published novel—a mystery featuring an Austin-based detective named Tres Navarre.

that *Big Red Tequila* was going to get published," he said. "It just felt different than anything else I'd ever written, because the novel had practically forced me to write it. The idea took me by the throat and wouldn't let me go until the manuscript was done."

Big Red Tequila did not just get published; it was a hit. Kate asked Rick to write another book about Tres Navarre. And another. Each year for the next seven years, Rick wrote another installment. He had a loyal fan base that expected a new episode every twelve months. Rick's books about Tres swept the awards given to mystery novels—the Anthony Award, the Shamus, the Edgar. "His books won every award they were eligible for," Kate recalled.

During the years when he was writing about Tres Navarre, another wonderful thing happened to Rick: he became a father. His first son, Haley, was born in 1994. His second son, Patrick, followed three years later. After eight years in California, Rick and Becky decided to return to San Antonio, where Rick's mom, Lyn, still lived, and where Rick had gotten a job at Saint Mary's Hall, a private school. He planned to write more about Tres Navarre. And he might still be writing about Tres Navarre today if it hadn't been for Haley, who asked for a bedtime story and liked it so much that he convinced his dad to write it down.

The success of the Percy Jackson books has made Rick, posing here at the British Museum, an international star.

Chapter 2
A HERO IS BORN

Haley (the Irish word for "ingenious") Riordan grew up to be a voracious reader. And by age sixteen, he was writing manuscripts longer than his father's!

But when Haley started school, he had some trouble focusing in the classroom. He was tested for attention deficit/hyperactivity disorder (ADHD) and dyslexia. Haley was frustrated and worried that the testing meant something was wrong with him. "We had to explain to him that the testing was designed to help the teachers help him, not to make him feel bad," Rick remembered.

Because reading was initially a struggle, Rick read aloud to Haley—something that Rick suggests all parents do no matter how well their children read. Haley was fascinated by Greek myths, so Rick recounted all the ones he knew well from having taught mythology to middle school English students.

"When I ran out of myths, he was disappointed, and asked me if I could make up something new with the same characters," Rick recalled. "I remembered a creative writing project I used to do with my sixth graders: I would let them create their own demigod hero, the son or daughter of any god they wanted, and have them describe a Greek-style quest for that hero. Off the top of my head, I made up Percy Jackson [Jackson is a family name] and told Haley all about his quest to recover Zeus's lightning bolt in modern-day America."

It took Rick several nights to tell the whole story, but Haley didn't mind; he was riveted. When Rick finished, Haley had some advice for his dad: he should make Percy Jackson's story into a book. If you look at it this way, Percy Jackson's real father isn't Poseidon; it's Haley Riordan. After all, it was Haley's idea to put Percy's adventures into print!

Rick resisted at first. He had a lot to do already—he was trying to write a new Tres Navarre book while teaching full-time. But he thought Haley's idea was a good one. "I somehow found the time to write the first Percy Jackson book over the next year," Rick said. "I just really enjoyed writing it. The story was such fun, and so different from my adult fiction, that I found myself spending a lot of time on it."

Part of the new story's appeal for Rick—and for his readers—is that Percy is a very unlikely superhero. Like Haley, Percy has dyslexia and ADHD. He has never gotten a grade higher than a C, and he thinks he's a loser. But soon after his adventures at Camp Half-Blood begin, Percy learns that his difficulties in school are not weaknesses after all, but sure signs of greatness. Words on a page seem jumbled to Percy because his mind is hardwired for ancient Greek. It's not ADHD that makes it hard for Percy to sit still; it's a hyper-awareness that he'll need later to keep himself alive in battle.

Rick likes to stress that dyslexia and ADHD are not necessarily just disabilities. They can turn into strengths instead of weaknesses later in life. "ADHD/dyslexic kids tend to be extremely articulate and fun to be around. Above all, they are creative thinkers, because they have been forced to find unorthodox ways to solve problems their entire school

The fictional Camp Half-Blood, a secret demigod training facility, inspired real summer camps for Percy Jackson fans in several states. At this New York camp, kids listen to the rules for a game of Capture the Flag.

RICK'S TIPS FOR KIDS WHO DON'T LIKE TO READ

When Haley Riordan was diagnosed with ADHD, Rick began a new educational program himself: learning everything he could about the disorder that was keeping his son from succeeding in school. Rick recommends two books for parents in a similar situation: *Keeping a Head in School* by Mel Levine and *Driven to Distraction* by Edward Hallowell and John Ratey. Rick also figured out some ways to keep Haley interested in reading, even when it was a challenge:

- **Read together.** The next time a grownup tells you to get a book, ask them to get a book and join you! Adults who read wind up having children who read.

- **The right book at the right time.** Find reading material that matches your interest. It may not even be a book; instead, it might be a magazine about cars or sports. It's still reading even if it isn't a novel.

- **Limit distractions.** Reading with TV or music on is probably not a good idea. Still, many kids need something to fiddle with while they are trying to read. Rick suggests a "stress ball, eraser, or some other small object to absorb their energy."

career," Rick told an interviewer in 2007. "This makes them highly valuable employees once they find a career that engages their interest."

After Rick finished *The Lightning Thief*, the first book in the Percy Jackson series, he read it aloud to Haley, who loved it—again. But Rick felt he also needed readers who weren't related to him to confirm Haley's opinion.

Rick said, "I wanted to be sure it would interest older kids—the middle school ages that I taught. I picked a few of my sixth, seventh, and eighth graders and asked them if they'd be willing to 'test drive' the novel. I was nervous! I'm used to showing my work to adults, but I had no idea if kids would like Percy. I finally understood what it must be like for them, turning in an essay to me and waiting to get their grades back!"

Fortunately for Rick, his students *did* like the novel, but they had some suggestions. First, they told him that his original title, *Son of the Sea God*, gave away the mystery of Percy's father. Next, one student helped Rick refine the way Percy's sword, Anaklusmos, works. "But they let me know in no uncertain terms that they thought it should be published," Rick said.

Now Rick just had to find an editor who liked his manuscript as much as his students did.

Logan Lerman starred as Percy Jackson in the 2010 film adaptation of *The Lightning Thief.*

Chapter 3
BEST-SELLERDOM

It turns out that finding the time to write *The Lightning Thief* was harder than finding a publisher. Nancy Gallt, the literary agent who received the letter from Ransom Reese, held an auction to sell the manuscript and had multiple bidders vying for the right to become Percy Jackson's publisher.

"I knew it had a lot of potential," Gallt said. "I thought, 'This could do for Greek gods what Harry Potter did for wizards.' What was astonishing was that nobody had come up with this idea before, because it's a natural marriage of Greek mythology and modern adventure. The Greek myths have been a continual source for novelists for centuries, but nobody had thought to bring it into the modern world."

Gallt was so sold on Rick's idea that she was able to sell a sequel to *The Lightning Thief* before Rick even wrote it.

Though Gallt's enthusiasm proved to be well founded, *The Lightning Thief* wasn't an instant success. Despite the old axiom, "Don't judge a book by its cover," many readers do, and the first jacket cover of *The Lightning Thief* sported a mishmash of confusing elements. Moreover, at 375 pages, *The Lightning Thief* was considered a bit daunting for some of the reluctant readers Rick was trying to reach.

Illustrator John Rocco, who won a 2012 Caldecott Honor for his picture book *Blackout*, redesigned the cover for the paperback editions of the Percy Jackson books.

The reviews were terrific, however. The *New York Times* praised *The Lightning Thief* as "perfectly paced, with electrifying moments chasing each other like heartbeats." Rick's novel received a starred review in *School Library Journal,* and *Publishers Weekly* predicted that "this swift and humorous adventure will leave many readers eager for the next installment."

The reviews brought Rick's novel to the attention of Hollywood. The major corporation 20th Century Fox purchased the film rights to *The Lightning Thief* before the book ever appeared on a best-seller list or won an award.

Rick's publisher, Disney/Hyperion Books, knew kids would love Percy if they found his story. So executive Brenda Bowen asked an illustrator to create a different cover for the sequel, *The Sea of Monsters*, and a matching jacket for the paperback edition of *The Lightning Thief*. These covers, designed by John Rocco, were a hit with booksellers, librarians, and kids.

"The second time was the charm," said Nancy Gallt. "After the new covers, that's when the book really started to take off."

Rick also credits librarians—especially those in the Lone Star State—with helping him find an audience.

"It has been especially thrilling to watch Rick's rise in popularity," said Texas librarian Jeanette Larson, who has known Riordan for more than two decades and has promoted his books at workshops for school and public libraries. "When I talk about popular books and how many copies of some books a library will need to buy, I used to use Harry Potter as an example. Now I use Rick's books as the example."

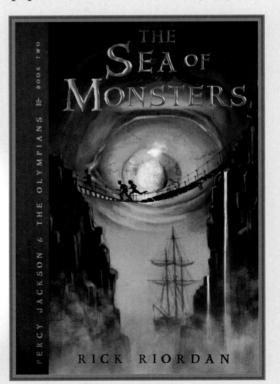

One of the goals of the redesign was to create a unified design for all of the books in the Percy Jackson and the Olympians series.

IT'S ALL GREEK TO RICK

Rick's favorite Greek myth when he was a kid: "Jason and the Argonauts"

Rick's favorite character from his own books: Tyson the Cyclops (although this changes from time to time)

Cabin Rick would live in at Camp Half-Blood: Hermes, definitely. That's where all the action is!

By the end of 2006, Percy Jackson was becoming a household name outside of Texas as well. *The Sea of Monsters* was named a *Child* Magazine Best Book of the Year and became a national best seller.

The series was getting more popular with each installment. The third title, *The Titan's Curse*, reached the top spot on the *New York Times* best-seller list, and the fourth title, *The Battle of the Labyrinth,* had a first printing of one million copies.

Even before the release of the fifth and final book, *The Last Olympian*, readers began begging Rick not to end Percy's story, but Rick felt that it was time to turn his attention to other ideas he hadn't had time to work on. "All good things must end, guys!" he wrote on his blog.

As he finished the series that had made him famous, Rick's thoughts turned to the woman he felt had made his life as a writer possible. The dedication to *The Last Olympian* reads as follows:

> To Mrs. Pabst, my eighth grade English teacher, who started me on my journey as a writer

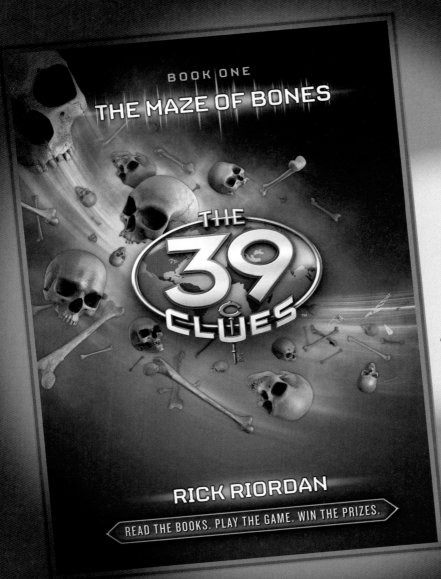

BOOK ONE

THE MAZE OF BONES

THE 39 CLUES™

RICK RIORDAN

READ THE BOOKS. PLAY THE GAME. WIN THE PRIZES.

Rick wrote the first installment in the 10-book series about Amy and Dan Cahill, who must follow cryptic clues around the globe in search of a mysterious fortune.

Chapter 4
ONE DOOR CLOSES AND ANOTHER OPENS

The success of the Percy Jackson books meant that Rick had to put aside his Tres Navarre series for a while. He was in demand on many fronts. Even while he was still finishing Percy's story, kids began asking him to write a similar series based on Egyptian mythology. Rick also had agreed to be the lead writer for a series from Scholastic called the 39 Clues, which would have an online, interactive component. Rick wrote an outline for the entire series and authored the first book, *The Maze of Bones,* which became another number one *New York Times* best seller.

Something had to give, however. Rick reluctantly decided to quit his job teaching middle school.

"It was a hard decision. I love teaching. I love working with kids," Rick said. "I just didn't think I'd be able to meet all my deadlines and do a good job in the classroom."

Since making that decision, Rick has been writing full-time and continuing to produce best-selling, kid-pleasing novels. After finishing Percy Jackson's story, he turned his attention to Egyptian mythology with the Kane Chronicles, a trilogy about a brother and sister who are raised separately but whose shared ancestry goes back to the pharaohs.

"As I talked to kids across the country, the one area they were all interested in and that fired their imaginations was ancient Egypt," Rick said. "Part of my philosophy as a teacher and writer is to pay attention to them. I took their ideas seriously. Then it was a matter of figuring out the premise, to make it funny, modern, and relevant for kids. That's the challenge I'd had as a teacher: this happened three thousand years ago; why should I care? How is it relevant to me? How can I make kids part of it and make it matter in a meaningful way?"

The first book in the series, *The Red Pyramid*, introduces Carter and Sadie Kane. Sadie, who is twelve, is being raised in London by her late

Rick autographs a copy of *The Red Pyramid* at a party held at the Brooklyn Museum in New York to launch the Kane Chronicles series.

mother's parents. Carter, who is fourteen, is being raised by his dad, an Egyptologist. Like Haley Riordan, Carter is homeschooled.

"It was important to me that the book have two narrators, one boy and one girl," Rick said. "Although the Percy Jackson books have been touted as 'boy books,' that's not what I see at events; the audience is usually about half and half, boys and girls."

In between writing the books in the Kane Chronicles trilogy, Rick also made time to return to Camp Half-Blood with a third series, the Heroes of Olympus. "I had a ton of ideas from Greek mythology that I could not fit into the Percy Jackson series, and there were many other stories about the characters at Camp Half-Blood that I wanted to explore," Rick said. The first book, *The Lost Hero*, was released in October 2010, with a planned total of five books in the series. Readers made the book a hit immediately. In 2011, there were weeks when Rick did not just have one book on the national best-seller list; his books dominated the list! The second book in the Heroes of Olympus series, *The Son of Neptune*, was published in 2011, and the third, *The Mark of Athena*, was published in 2012. The fourth book, *The House of Hades*, is scheduled for release in late 2013. In addition, in 2012 Rick published a collection of short stories called *The Demigod Diaries* as a companion book to the Heroes of Olympus series.

It was no surprise, then, that at the 2011 Children's Choice Awards, Rick's name was called out—more than once. *"The Red Pyramid* won for best 5th–6th grade book, which was amazing enough," Rick wrote on his blog. "Then I was called up again when I won Author of the Year for *The Lost Hero*. Holy Hera!"

Many film critics compared the film version of *The Lightning Thief* to the Harry Potter movies and found it didn't have as much appeal.

Chapter 5
HOLLYWOOD!

Having a book made into a movie is usually an exciting event for an author, but it also has drawbacks. When authors sell the film rights to their books, they typically have to relinquish creative control to the movie studio that produces the film. In Rick's case, he received a version of the script and was invited to comment on it, but that was the extent of his involvement.

The movie opened in February 2010 and was a box-office disappointment, earning less in the United States than it had cost to make. Many kids were unhappy with the producers' decision to make some key characters (including Percy) many years older in the film than they are in the book. Casting children and even teenage actors in a film is tricky because most young actors don't have enough experience to carry a starring role, and very few have the name recognition that attracts fans during the movie's crucial opening weekend. Whatever the producers' reasons, this choice didn't sit well with the tweens and teens who had made the book into a best seller.

That said, the release of the film increased public awareness of the Percy Jackson series. "Although it wasn't faithful to the book, it was a ninety-minute advertisement for the book," said Rick's agent, Nancy

The actor Pierce Brosnan, whose film credits include a stint as James Bond, played Chiron, one of Percy's camp counselors, in *The Lightning Thief.*

Gallt. "It was a huge help, frankly, in making a Rick an international presence." As it turned out, the film performed better internationally than it did in the United States, and this allowed the producers to recoup the cost of making it.

Reporters repeatedly asked Rick to comment on the film when it was released, but he had a very good reason not to: he hadn't seen it. "He was continuing to write about Camp Half-Blood and Percy Jackson, and he said he would rather have the images of those places he'd created in his head than how somebody else imagined it," Gallt said. "He didn't want to be writing about Chiron and have the face of [actor] Pierce Brosnan come to mind."

Despite the poor performance of the first movie, *The Sea of Monsters* has been filmed and is scheduled for release in August 2013. In addition, film rights for the 39 Clues series have been purchased by the famous director Steven Spielberg!

Filmmakers used the technique known as CGI to make it appear that the actress Uma Thurman, who played the Greek goddess Medusa, had a head full of snakes instead of hair.

Rick, with his editor Stephanie Owens Lurie, met booksellers at the 2011 Book Expo America convention in New York.

Chapter 6
WHAT'S NEXT FOR RICK?

As of 2013, there were more than 15 million copies of Rick's books in print. Kids are reading his books all over the world; they have been reprinted in as many as thirty-five languages, including Portuguese, Hebrew, Spanish, Italian, German, Chinese, and, of course, Greek! But Rick has not been resting on his laurels—he has signed book contracts that will keep him busy until at least 2017.

And although Rick has left the classroom, in many ways his teaching has simply taken a different form: reinvigorating classic myths for a student body that has grown exponentially larger than he ever could have reached had he continued to work at a school.

"The good part is, I still get to work with kids as a children's author," Rick said. "Hopefully, I'll be able to get more kids interested in reading mythology with my books than I ever did as a teacher."

Indeed, Rick says he's heard that many schools have incorporated *The Lightning Thief* into their curricula and that high school teachers are using the books as a gateway into Homer's *Iliad* and *Odyssey*. "I've had letters from librarians who said, 'My 200s (the Dewey decimal system's classification for world religions) were gathering dust and now I can't keep them on the shelf.'"

"Writing for kids suits both sides of [Rick's] life—his life as a writer and his life as a teacher," said Nancy Gallt. "It surprises him that it took him so long to figure that out."

Maybe someday Rick will get back to writing about his first character, the detective Tres Navarre. After all, he still owes Kate Miciak, his editor at Bantam Dell, one more book.

"He sort of started it, but I believe his plate is very full right now," Kate said. "And I think those Percy Jackson fans would break my kneecaps if I asked him for [the next Tres book]."

Kate doesn't mind, though. She's also a Percy fan—and, most of all, a Rick Riordan fan: "We are so thrilled he found this huge audience and this great platform. Every time he wins an award or I see his name on the *New York Times* best-seller list, I think, 'There's my kid.'"

In between writing new installments of the Kane Chronicles, Rick produced a series about life at Camp Half-Blood. He introduced the first volume, *The Lost Hero*, before fans in Austin, Texas, in 2010.

RICK'S TIPS FOR ASPIRING WRITERS

* Find a mentor who believes in your talent. So don't be afraid to ask for help!

* Read a lot! You will learn the craft of writing by immersing yourself in the voices, styles, and structures of other writers.

* Write every day! Keep a journal. Jot down interesting stories you heard. Write descriptions of people you see. It doesn't really matter what you write, but you must practice. Writing is like a sport—if you don't practice, the writing muscles atrophy [waste away].

* Don't get discouraged! Rejection is a part of writing. The trick is to keep at it. Wallpaper your room with rejection notes, if you want, but don't give up.

Rick says that being a best-selling author is great, but the real reward comes in reaching individual readers, especially those who, like him, initially had trouble connecting with books: "I measure success by anecdotes—the kid who told me he never liked books until he found *The Lightning Thief*, the parent who thanked me for turning her daughter into a reader, the teacher who said I turned her class around because they bonded over reading Percy Jackson every day. That's what it's all about for me."

RICK LIKES TO READ:

Rick says that the ultimate payback for avoiding reading while he was a kid was growing up to be an English teacher who had to convince his students to do the assigned reading. These are some of the books that he actually did read and enjoy as a boy.

Fletcher and Zenobia by Victoria Chess, illustrated by Edward Gorey

The Golden Fleece and the Heroes Who Lived before Achilles by Padraic Colum

The Greek Gods by Bernard Evslin

James and the Giant Peach by Roald Dahl

The Fellowship of the Ring by J. R. R. Tolkien

The Xanth series by Piers Anthony

BOOKS BY RICK RIORDAN

PERCY JACKSON AND THE OLYMPIANS SERIES

The Lightning Thief (Hyperion, 2005)

The Sea of Monsters (Hyperion, 2006)

The Titan's Curse (Hyperion, 2007)

The Battle of the Labyrinth (Hyperion, 2008)

The Last Olympian (Hyperion, 2009)

THE HEROES OF OLYMPUS SERIES

The Lost Hero (Hyperion, 2010)

The Son of Neptune (Hyperion, 2011)

The Mark of Athena (Hyperion, 2012)

COMPANION BOOKS

The Demigod Files (Hyperion, 2009)

Demigods and Monsters (Hyperion, 2009)

Percy Jackson and the Olympians: The Ultimate Guide (Hyperion, 2010)

The Demigod Diaries, (Hyperion, 2012)

THE 39 CLUES SERIES

The Maze of Bones (Scholastic, 2008)

Vespers Rising (Scholastic, 2011)

THE KANE CHRONICLES SERIES

The Red Pyramid (Hyperion, 2010)

The Throne of Fire (Hyperion, 2011)

The Serpent's Shadow (Hyperion, 2012)

GLOSSARY

attention deficit/hyperactivity disorder (ADHD)—A brain impairment that affects one's ability to concentrate and stay focused.

axiom—A statement or idea that people generally accept as true.

Dewey decimal system—A library classification system developed by Melvil Dewey in 1876. The system organizes books on shelves in a specific order that makes it easy to find a book and return it to its proper place.

dyslexia—An impairment of the brain that interferes with one's ability to read.

master's thesis—A lengthy academic paper based on original research, usually required in order to earn an advanced academic degree.

optioned—Acquired the rights to a book or play for the purposes of adapting it into a screenplay, usually for a designated period of time, after which the rights to the property return to the original owner or author.

pseudonym—A fake name, often used by a writer to hide his or her real identity.

query letter—A letter written by an author to an agent or publisher. In the letter, the author asks about the agent or publisher's interest in seeing or buying a particular manuscript.

CHRONOLOGY

June 5, 1964: Richard Russell Riordan Jr. is born in San Antonio, Texas.

1982: Rick graduates from Alamo Heights High School.

1986: Rick graduates from the University of Texas at Austin with a double major in English and history.

1988: Rick takes his first teaching job in New Braunfels, Texas.

1989: Rick and his wife, Becky, move to California, where Rick begins graduate school at San Francisco State University.

1994: Rick's son Haley is born.

1997: Rick's first novel, *Big Red Tequila*, written for adults, is published. The Riordans move back to San Antonio, where Rick works at Saint Mary's Hall, a private Episcopal school for grades K to twelve.

1998: Rick's son Patrick is born.

2002: Rick is given Saint Mary's Hall's first Master Teacher Award.

2003: Rick is inducted into the Texas Institute of Letters.

2004: *The Lightning Thief* is published by Disney/Hyperion Press.

2005: Rick quits his teaching job in order to write full-time.

February 2010: The movie version of *The Lightning Thief* is released.

2011: *The Red Pyramid* wins the Children's Choice Award; Riordan is also named Author of the Year for *The Lost Hero*.

FURTHER INFORMATION

Books

Are you interested in trying to write stories yourself? These two books offer guidance:

Levine, Gail Carson. *Writing Magic*. New York: Collins, 2006.

Messner, Kate. *Real Revision: Authors' Strategies to Share with Student Writers*. Portland, ME: Stenhouse, 2011.

Websites

Rick's website: www.rickriordan.com

Fans can follow Rick on Twitter: http://twitter.com/camphalfblood

Rick's blog, *Myth & Mystery,* can be found at http://rickriordan.blogspot.com

Rick's publishers have created several websites devoted exclusively to his books:

Percy Jackson & the Olympians: www.percyjacksonbooks.com

The Kane Chronicles: http://disney.go.com/official-sites/kane-chronicles/index

The Heroes of Olympus: http://disney.go.com/disneybooks/heroes-of-olympus/

The 39 Clues: www.the39clues.com

BIBLIOGRAPHY

A note to report writers from Sue Corbett

To write this biography, I read all of Rick's books and did research online by reading articles that other journalists have written about Rick. I had interviewed Rick myself several times in my role as the children's book reviewer for the *Miami Herald*. I also spoke to Rick's editor, booksellers, and librarians.

Below is a list of sources that I used. Anytime *you* write a report, you should also keep track of where you got your information. It is fine to use information in your report if you found it somewhere else, as long as you give the source credit in a footnote, endnote, or note within the report itself. (Your teacher can tell you how he or she prefers you to list your sources.)

It is not okay to pass off other people's work as your own.

PRINT ARTICLES

"The Greek Revival," by Sue Corbett, *Miami Herald,* May 14, 2009.

"Percy Jackson: My Boy's Own Adventure," by Sally Williams, *The Guardian,* Feb. 6, 2010.

"Rick Riordan on Four Ways to Get Kids with ADHD to Read," by Rick Riordan, *The Wall Street Journal*, Oct. 15, 2010.

"Talking with Rick Riordan," by Jeanette Larson, Book Links, May 2009, pp. 18–20.

ONLINE SOURCES

"Rick Riordan: The World as His Classroom," by Jennifer M. Brown. ShelfAwareness.com, May 4, 2010.

"Biography," http://www.rickriordan.com/about-rick/biography.aspx.

WBBT: Rick Riordan Interview, Jen Robinson's Book Page, http://jkrbooks. typepad.com/blog/2007/11/wbbt-rick-riord.html.

"A video interview with Rick Riordan," Adlit.org, http://www.adlit.org/ articles/authors/riordan.

INDEX

Anthony Award, 15
aspiring writers, tips for, 39
attention deficit hyperactivity disorder (ADHD), 17, 18, 21
awards and honors, 5, 15, 31

Battle of the Labyrinth, The (Riordan), 26, 41
Belisle, Lyn, 9, 15
best-seller lists, 26, 29, 31
Big Red Tequila (Riordan), 13–15, **14**, 41
book reviews, 24
books, recommended, 40
Bowen, Brenda, 24–25
Brosnan, Pierce, **34**

Camp Half-Blood, 12, **12**, 18, **19**, 31
characters
    Carter Kane (character), 31
    Jackson "Tres" Navarre (character), 13, 38
    Percy Jackson (character), 18
    Sadie Kane (character), 30–31
    Tyson the Cyclops (character), 26
childhood, 9–11
Children's Choice Awards, 31
Chronology, 43
college career, 11–13
cover art, 23, **24**, 24–25, **25**

Demigod Diaries, The (Riordan), 41
Demigod Files, The (Riordan), 41
Demigods and Monsters (Riordan), 41
Driven to Distraction (Hallowell and Ratey), 20
dyslexia, 17, 18, 21

Edgar Award, 5, 15
education, 9–13, 37
Egyptian mythology, 29
employment, as teacher, 13, 15, 29

Fellowship of the Ring, The (Tolkien), 40
film rights, 24, 33, 35
Fletcher and Zenobia (Chess), 40

Gallt, Nancy, 4–7, 23, 25, 33–34
Golden Fleece and the Heroes Who Lived before Achilles (Colum), 40
Greek Gods, The (Evslin), 40
Greek mythology, 17–18, 26, 31, 37

Handler, Daniel, 7
Heroes of Olympus series (Riordan), 31, 41
Hobbit, The (Tolkien), **10**, 10–11

inspiration, for writing, 13, 15, 17–18, 39

Jackson "Tres" Navarre (character), 13, 38
James and the Giant Peach (Dahl), 40
"Jason and the Argonauts" (myth), 26
journals, keeping, 39

Kane Chronicles series, 29–31, 41
Keeping a Head in School (Levine), 20

Last Olympian, The (Riordan), 26–27, 41
Lerman, Logan, **22**
librarians, 25, 37
Lightning Thief, The (Riordan), 41

cover art, **24**
movie of, **22**, 24, **32**, 33–35
publication process, 4–7, 23–25
writing process and, 17–18
literary agents, 4–7, 13–14, 23
Lord of the Rings trilogy (Tolkien), 10–11, 40
Lost Hero, The (Riordan), 31, 41

Mark of Athena, The (Riordan), 31, 41
marriage and children, 13, 15, 17–18, 21
Maze of Bones, The (Riordan), **28**, 41
mentors, 39
Miciak, Kate, 14, 15, 38
movie, of *The Lightning Thief*, **22**, 24, **32**, 33–35
mystery novels, 5, 13–15, 38, 41

Pabst, Patricia, 10–11, 27
Percy Jackson (character), 18
Percy Jackson and the Olympians: The Ultimate Guide (Riordan), 41
personal life
    childhood, 9–11
    college career, 11–13
    marriage and children, 13, 15, 17–18, 21
popularity, growth of, 25, 26–27
pseudonyms, 4–7
publication process, 4–7, 11, 13–15, 23–25

query letters, 5–6

reading, enjoyment of, 10–11
reading strategies, 20, 39
Red Pyramid, The (Riordan), **30**, 30–31, 41

Reese, Ransom, 4–7
rejection letters, 11, 39
reluctant readers, 10–11, 20, 39
reports, writing, 45
reviews, 24, 33
Riordan, Becky, 13, 15
Riordan, Haley, 15, 17–18, 20, 21, 31
Riordan, Patrick, 15
Riordan, Richard, Sr., 9
Rocco, John, **24**, 25

Sadie Kane (character), 30–31
sales, 37
Sea of Monsters, The (Riordan), **25**, 35, 41
Serpent's Shadow, The (Riordan), 41
Shamus Award, 15
short stories, 11, 13
Snicket, Lemony, 7
Son of Neptune, The (Riordan), 31, 41
Spielberg, Steven, 35
summer camps, 12, **12**, **19**

teaching career, 13, 15, 29, 37
39 Clues series (Riordan), **28**, 29, 35, 41
Throne of Fire, The (Riordan), 41
Thurman, Uma, **35**
Titan's Curse, The (Riordan), 26, 41
Tyson the Cyclops (character), 26

Vespers Rising (Riordan), 41

writing process, 17–18, 29, 39

Xanth series (Anthony), 40

ABOUT THE AUTHOR:

Sue Corbett is a reporter who has worked for the *Miami Herald*, *People* magazine, and *Publishers Weekly*. She is also the author of several novels for kids, including *The Last Newspaper Boy in America*, *Free Baseball*, and *12 Again*.